CW00684749

SWOT Anal

A guide to SWOT for
students of business studies

SWOT Analysis

A guide to SWOT for
students of business studies

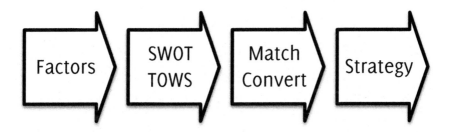

Notice of Rights

All rights reserved. No part of this book may be reproduced, sold, copied, or transmitted by any means without the permission of the copyright holder and the publisher.

Brief quotations may be used in a book review or a scholarly pursuit. For permissions, please contact the Leadership Library by email to: editor@leadership-library.co.uk

First printing: November 2016
Language <en-gb>
ISBN 978-0-9932504-2-2

The Leadership Library is an imprint of Spectaris Limited. Registered in England: 05448422

www.leadership-library.co.uk

Copyright

Copyright © 2016 Alan Sarsby
Alan Sarsby asserts his rights under the Copyright, Designs and Patents Act 1988 to be identified as the author of this work.

Notice of liability

Reasonable steps have been taken in the preparation of this work; it is based substantially on the real-world experience of the author. The opinions and suggestions expressed are those of the author alone and do not constitute legal advice, are not instructions, nor commands. You alone are accountable for complying with the law in your jurisdiction.
The information contained in this work and associated resources is offered on an "as is" basis without warranty.

While reasonable steps have been taken in the preparation of this guide, neither the author nor the publishers shall have any liability to any person or entity regarding any loss or damage caused or alleged to be caused directly or indirectly by the information contained herein.
The application of any methods, ideas, or suggestions in this work is at your risk.

Trademarks

All trademarks are acknowledged as the property of their owners and are used in this publication in an editorial sense.

Third parties

Mention of, or links to, third parties are given in good faith as a convenience and are NOT in any way whatsoever an endorsement nor recommendation.
Links change over time; no guarantees can be given that they work at the time of your reading.

GM102a005.zrtf

Foreword

You've been given a SWOT based assignment by your tutor or supervisor; now what? The SWOT framework looks deceptively simple so it should be a straightforward assignment; how hard can it be?

Good guidance is hard to find. Sources one would assume are of high quality frequently make errors in their explanations. Consequently the analysis is flawed.

The requirements for academic purposes (reflected in the marking scheme) usually fall into a pattern similar to the following:

- Demonstrate your understanding of the critical theory;

- Gather data from a case-study or a field trip;

- Apply the data to the SWOT framework;

- Deduce the findings;

- Draw conclusions and make recommendations.

With this in mind, this book is organised as

Part 1   The critical theory

Part 2   Planning and preparation for your assignment

Part 3   Demonstrating SWOT using short case studies

Contents

Part 1 — Theory

1 Introducing SWOT

1.1 The four boxes

SWOT is a popular 4-box strategy analysis and strategy development framework. The acronym SWOT is derived from:

- Strengths
- Weaknesses
- Opportunities
- Threats

SWOT has been around for decades and could lay claim to being the most widely used strategy tool in modern times. It is used by industry, commerce, and charitable and voluntary organisations. In higher education, SWOT is often in the curriculum of business studies and strategy training courses . If you have ever applied for a business bank loan, it is likely that the bank would want to see a SWOT analysis or something similar.

Advantages — SWOT has many advantages, a few of which are:

- SWOT is easy to understand — a simple diagram and no mathematics.
- SWOT is applicable to many levels in an organisation — from an individual, a team, a business unit or division, and the corporate strategy.
- SWOT can be applied at different depths — lightweight treatment for simpler circumstances, through to highly detailed treatment for larger or complex issues.
- SWOT is highly visual, consequently easy to communicate to other stakeholders.

Disadvantages — Despite its popularity and the advantages above, SWOT has several disadvantages. A few of these include:

- Using poor quality data including anecdotes, hearsay, and factors expressed as generalisations.
- Using data which is biased by perceptions, beliefs, personality types and preferences.
- Not separating the analysis elements of data collection, its evaluation, and the consequent decision-making.
- It is easy to ignore the underlying principles which leads to factors being assigned to the wrong area of analysis — and consequently resulting in an invalid strategy.

1.2   Does SWOT lead to a strategy?

SWOT, by itself, does not lead to a strategy. It is an analysis and development tool; tools are only as good as their operator. You still have to do the work, interpret the analysis, and make the decisions.

When used well, SWOT is a useful *tool* to *aid* to your thinking. However, it is dangerously easy to undertake a SWOT analysis that does not result in a strategy. Frequently the failure is from two causes: often due to a lack of understanding of what a strategy is; and using SWOT erroneously.

	For our purpose of this work, a strategy gives you an advantage or a point of distinction.

1.3   Literature review

A literature review using internet search engines return approximately twenty-million results for the term 'SWOT' — far too much to summarise here. Instead, a short history of SWOT and references/citations is included in Appendix 5 and the bibliography, these may be helpful in your assignment.

2 The SWOT framework

2.1 Illustrating SWOT

SWOT should be drawn as shown in Figure 1. You can be creative about how it is drawn and some variations are shown in Appendix 1.

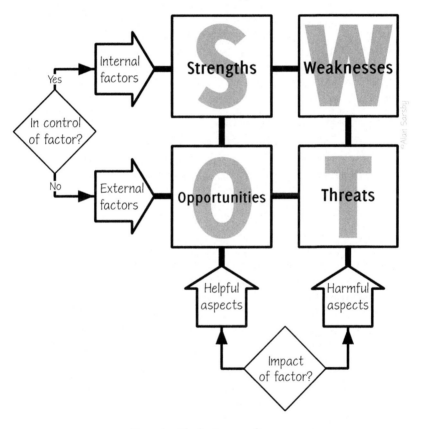

Figure 1: The basic SWOT diagram

The axes are important in SWOT because they define the content of the four boxes, S (Strengths), W (Weaknesses), O (Opportunities), and T (Threats). If the axes are omitted; problems often arise when collecting and assigning information to the appropriate quadrant. .

2.2   SWOT terminology

SWOT has its own nomenclature, or jargon. The basic vocabulary includes:

> **Factor** — A *factor* is relevant data or information. SWOT is
> predominately a data and information gathering framework which
> records *input* factors. In practical use, the four boxes each hold a list
> of factors, often as a bullet-point list with supporting documentation.

The rows in the SWOT diagram (Figure 1), distinguish between the factors you
control, and those factors you do not control (or cannot control). In SWOT
jargon, the factors you control are *Internal factors*, and those you do not
control are *External factors*.

> **Internal factors** — Internal factors are those that you or your
> organisation have control over.
> Strengths and Weaknesses are internal factors.

> **External factors** — External factors are those which you or your
> organisation has little or no control over.
> Opportunities and Threats are external factors.

The columns in the SWOT diagram distinguish between factors that are
helpful, and those that are *harmful* in respect of your SWOT objective.

Helpful factors
Helpful factors are those that assist your success.
Strengths and Opportunities are helpful.

Harmful factors
Harmful factors are those that impede or block your success.
Weaknesses and Threats are harmful.

| | Whether a factor is helpful or harmful depends on the context, or objective, of your SWOT analysis. |

2.3   SWOT quadrants

Strengths

Strengths are *internal* and *helpful* in respect of the SWOT objective.
Strengths are factors that support an Opportunity or overcome a Threat.
Strengths might include:

- Financial strengths: robust balance sheet, cash flow, credit rating.
- Technological advantages: plant, machines, know-how.
- Customer services: in marketing, sales, service, reputation.
- People: talented, dedicated, skilled, well-trained.

Weaknesses

Weaknesses are *internal* and *harmful* in respect of the SWOT objective.
Weaknesses are factors that result in being unable to take advantage of an
opportunity, or are vulnerable to a Threat. Weaknesses might include:

- Financial weaknesses such as a high debt-liquidity ratio.
- Old or inflexible technology or processes.
- Customer service weaknesses, for example, long delivery times or
  poor customer communications.
- Skills shortages or poor employee morale.

Opportunities

Opportunities are *external* and *helpful* factors over which you have no
control but could be helpful. Opportunities arise from many sources, for
example:

- Competitors withdrawing from, or entering, the market.
- New social trends.
- Technological innovations.
- Restrictive legislation which can be viewed as an opportunity if it is
  a threat to your competition.

Opportunities can be tangible, such as new products, or intangible such as
enhanced reputation.

Threats

Threats are *external* and *harmful* factors over which you have no control. Threats are also tangible or intangible. A tangible threat could be a hostile takeover bid, new competitors, or theft. Intangible threats include, potential loss of reputation or brand damaging factors.

2.4   Context

Whether a factor is a Strength or a Weakness, and likewise whether a factor is an Opportunity or a Threat, depends on the context and purpose of the SWOT analysis. Context is vitally important in a SWOT analysis; this is covered in more detail in §5.1.

2.5   Summary

In this section we've introduced the basic components of SWOT. It is a straightforward framework, but with its apparent simplicity it is tempting to bypass the underlying principles and consequently end up without a worthwhile result.

To summarise what we have so far:

Axes
The axes are important to SWOT. The in control axis of Figure 1 defines the Internal or External factors; The impact axis defines Helpful or Harmful factors. Whether that factor is in the correct place depends on the context.

Context
A specific context is essential for a good quality SWOT; your Strength in one Context could be a Weakness in another. Writing a purpose statement helps to keep the analysis relevant rather than generalised.

3 SWOT analysis

3.1 The analysis

It is tempting to start an analysis in the top-left box, the Strengths. If you do so, it is likely that you'll end up with a very long list of self-congratulatory strengths that have nothing to do with the opportunities or threats. It is much more meaningful to look for the external factors first, and then look for the internal factors that help or hinder.

In swot, the analysis is performed by applying the technique of *Matching* and *Converting.*

3.2 Matching

MATCHING connects the *external* factors — Opportunities and Threats — to the *internal* Strengths and Weaknesses.
Matching is illustrated in Figure 2.

3.3 Converting

CONVERTING is the changing a harmful factor into a helpful factor. The two convert options are:

i)   Could Threat factor be turned into a advantage by *converting* the Threat into an Opportunity?

ii) Could a Weakness factor be *converted* into Strength?

Converting is illustrated in Figure 3.

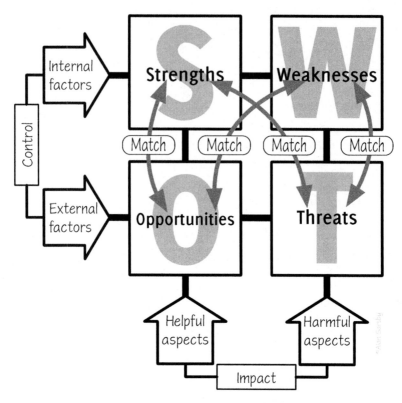

Figure 2: Potential Matching between internal and external factors

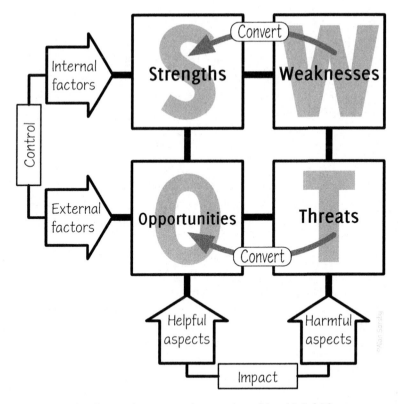

Figure 3:   Potential conversion between harmful and helpful factors

In preparation for later parts of this book, an example should help. The following example is a fast food business and we'll see how the context affects the decisions made following a SWOT analysis.

> Note — the label [Context] is introduced here because this notation is used to identify various components in the case studies.

The Basic Burger Bar

[Context] The Basic Burger Bar business is a fast-food restaurant. It is a town-centre retail business selling a small range of burgers and fries. Customers enter the premises then join a queue where they make their selection and are served immediately at the counter. Within a few minutes they have ordered, paid, and received their food. The food is delivered in a paper bag for takeaway ('to go' orders), or the same paper bag on a tray for 'eat-in' orders.

Customer travel time is quick, an 'eat-in' customer is unlikely to be in the burger bar for longer than 30 minutes. A 'to-go' (take-away) customer typically enters and leaves the restaurant within five minutes.

For 'eat-in' orders, customers take their tray to a table and consume their food with their fingers or a disposable fork. Afterwards they are expected to clear the table by taking the tray, with the trash, to a nearby collection point.

To illustrate matching, assume that you are the owner of the Basic Burger Bar and have commissioned some market research. The result of this research suggests that there is an opportunity for extending the menu to include plated food eaten with knives and forks.

Figure 4 illustrates how the Opportunity factors are *matched* to the Weakness factors.

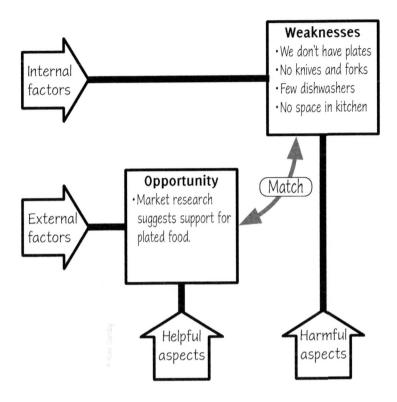

Figure 4: Matching an Opportunity to a Weakness for the Basic Burger Bar

Matching the external factor (demand for plated food) to the internal factors reveals some significant weaknesses.

Important: In this example, the absence of knifes and forks is a weakness only in the context of the opportunity for serving plated food.

4 SWOT becomes TOWS

4.1 Strategic responses

The SWOT framework shown in the earlier diagrams demonstrates its usefulness in recording factors. In a typical analysis project, each of the four boxes would contain a list of factors — often as a bullet-point list with supporting rationale in an accompanying document. These four SWOT lists are interesting as a *classification* of input factors, and using the analysis tools of *matching* and *converting* suggest, responses to a situation (the context) However, to advance our four lists of *input factors* into potential *strategic outputs*, the SWOT framework needs to be rearranged as shown in Figure 5.

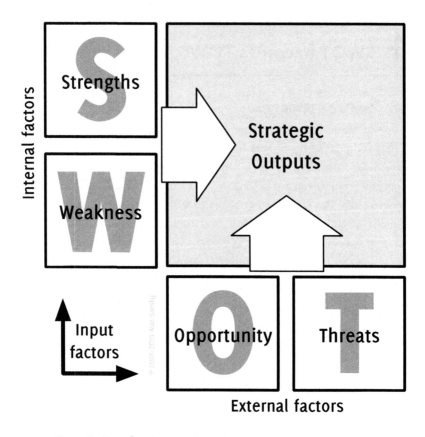

Figure 5: Transforming SWOT inputs into strategic responses – TOWS

In essence, SWOT has been turned inside out and the four input categories are
used to guide you towards *output* strategies or, if you prefer, strategic
responses. In this state the framework is usually known as TOWS (that is, SWOT
backwards).

4.2 The four generic strategies

The TOWS representation identifies four types of strategic response. The four approaches are illustrated in Figure 6. At each intersection between the internal and external factors a specific type of strategy .

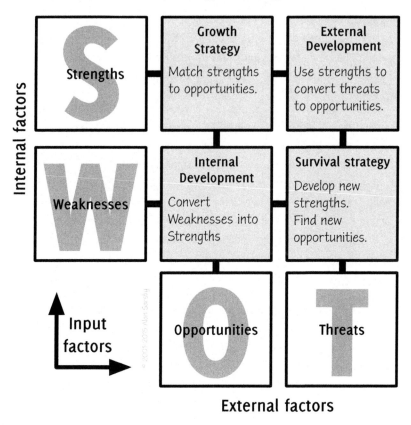

Figure 6: Specific types of response to the SWOT input factors

The characteristics of each generic strategy are:

Growth strategies (Opportunity × Strengths)

The essence of a growth-based strategy is to *Match* the Opportunity to your existing Strengths and do more of what you're already good at. A growth-based strategy usually involves investing in those factors that increase your capacity to do more of the same thing. The investment could include, for example, hiring extra people or procuring additional production machinery. The result of a growth-based strategy is continuation of your competitive advantage.

Internal development strategies (Opportunity × Weaknesses)

The main consideration in this type of strategy is to *Convert* weaknesses to strengths so they can be matched to an opportunity. An internal development strategy is about repairing or developing internal factors. The investment might include developing new skills, hiring new people with different skills or training existing people with new skills, designing new processes or developing new technology. The internal development strategy leads to new capabilities that were not present before, and these can be matched to an opportunity.

External development strategies (Threats × Strengths)

This type of strategy is based on using your existing strengths to *convert* a threat into an opportunity. An external development strategy might include extending your marketing reach into new areas or new customers through advertising; you might use skills in product development (a Strength) to broaden your services in existing markets.

Survival strategies (Threats × Weaknesses)

A threat and weaknesses combined — the worst possible scenario. Here you are faced with stark choices; for example, fundamentally change what your organisation is or does. Both match and convert are applicable here. Assuming that you choose to stay in business, the strategies are the simultaneous deployment of both External and Internal development actions.

5 Identifying SWOT factors

5.1 A context and purpose is essential

A factor might exist in several places on a swot analysis. To position a factor correctly within a swot analysis requires a context, objective, or purpose.

A few examples should demonstrate the importance of context.

- You might have skills in *using* off-the-shelf software, in which case the *skill* could be a Strength. However the software could be a Threat if it is mission-critical and the external developer doesn't include the functions that you need.

- Your proprietary software does what you want it to do, and hence might be a Strength. On the other hand, the cost of maintaining proprietary software might be expensive and hence a Weakness.

- Your billing system may be robust and reliable, satisfying regulatory standards for billing and invoicing; it is a Strength. But in the context of an Opportunity that requires flexible invoicing, your robust billing system might be a Weakness.

- A substantial cash reserve could be superficially seen as a Strength. However, this same cash reserve would make you an attractive take-over target in the context of a hostile business climate. So in that context, excess cash is a Weakness and potentially invites a Threat, possibly as a hostile takeover.

A good purpose statement is valuable because it helps to identify what inputs you need for the swot analysis. In a real situation, many swots exist side-by-side, each focusing on a specific issue or separate context.

By contrast, a SWOT without a context or purpose results in a generalised analysis with limited value. The data capture might be interesting, but without a context and purpose, the result is often somewhat vague statements masquerading as a strategy. A good SWOT analysis requires the overall context to be understood. Context helps to eliminate interesting but irrelevant actions.

The range of what might be a purpose is huge. The purpose could be formed around any of the business processes or functions. Classic business processes include, for example, invoicing, marketing, recruitment and product development. The purpose might also be to support one-off activities, for example mergers and acquisitions, bid and tender planning, or the formation of new internal business functions.

 A context and purpose are critical to the effective use of SWOT.

5.2   The environmental scan

In SWOT-based strategy development, the first step is known as an *environmental scan* — in plain English, what is going on around you.

Figure 7 shows some of the many sources that might contribute to an environmental scan. Both internal and external factors are included.

5.3   Identifying opportunities and threats

From the environmental scan external factors might be, for example, new legislation, a new competitor, or a gap in the market.

A popular nemonic known as PESTEL (Political, Economic, Social, Technological, Environmental and Legal) provides a checklist of issues and factors. Appendix 2 introduces the PESTEL model which helps with the discovery of external factors.

Each has a particular focus and benefit so you might need to use several — mix and match as needed.

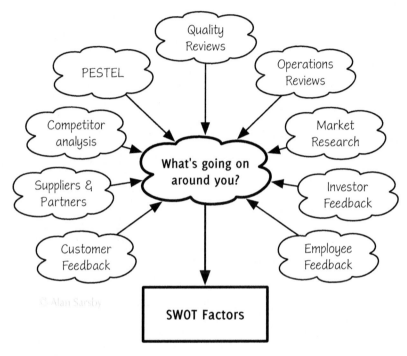

Figure 7: Sources of information for an environmental scan

5.4   Identifying strengths and weaknesses

Strengths and Weaknesses are internal factors over which you have control. You should look for these within your internal processes, your operations, and the way you do things (including your quality management systems, business ethos and culture). Appendix 3 illustrates three ways of identifying your Strengths and Weaknesses, including a suggested list of core business processes you could use as a checklist in your search for factors that help or hinder the external Opportunities or Threats.

Remember that factors classified as Strengths or Weaknesses are valid only within a given context or circumstance.

Part 2 — Preparation for the assignment

6 Strategy development

6.1 Application of SWOT in an assignment

Your assignment can be conveniently viewed as a self-contained project. A project has a beginning (with an objective or purpose), a middle (doing the work), and an end (submitting your assignment).

The basic approach follows a sequence:

- Clarify the context (the situation) and purpose of the analysis;

- Perform an environmental scan to gather data and information;

- Identify the Opportunities and Threats;

- Identify the Strengths and Weaknesses;

- Record the factors on a SWOT diagram;

- Match the Opportunities and Threats to the Strengths and Weaknesses;

- Consider how to convert harmful factors into helpful factors;

- Rearrange SWOT into a TOWS chart;

- Develop responses;

- Make choices and decisions; and

- Define actions to deploy the strategy.

A basic framework in [Referenced content is missing.] illustrates the type of method needed. You could treat this as an outline project plan, although you should modify this to suit your own circumstances.

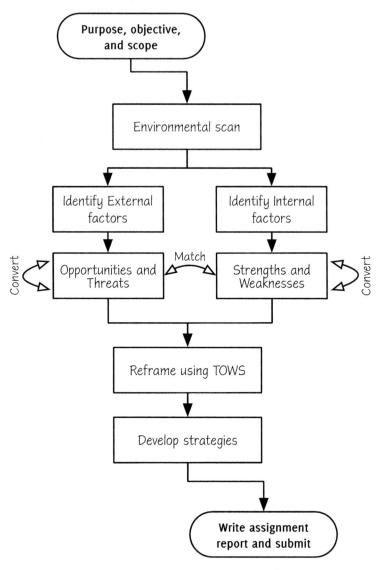

Figure 8: A suggested assignment plan SWOT/TOWS analysis

Although the method is shown as linear, the reality is that many feedback loops exist. For example, the analysis might show the need for an additional data source, so you will need to go back to the input factors.

6.2   Understand the environment and purpose of the analysis

We've already mentioned (§2.4) that context is important for SWOT analysis. The context enables you to assess and interpret the issues and factors so they are correctly located in the SWOT grid and therefore correctly considered in the TOWS formulation of strategic responses.

In SWOT, a context statement describes the environment within which the subject (business, organisation, etc) which is being studied. A context statement might include the following.

- What the business does, what it sells and who its typical customers are. For example, is the business a retail operation, or business-to-business; walk-in shop, Internet or phone; quick sales (fast moving goods) or bespoke. This element of the context is important when considering the business-fit of the strategies that emerge from the SWOT analysis.

- An indication of scale — are you a sole trader, a small business or a corporate?

- A summary of the environmental scan, — what are the issues the business facing. This element is a good leading in to the purpose of the analysis.

For SWOT to work well, the analysis needs a purpose. The good-quality purpose statement can be phrased as a direct question. The case studies following use this approach.

6.3   Use TOWS to select a strategic approach

Redrawing the earlier SWOT analysis of the Basic Burger Bar (Figure 4) into TOWS, positions the issue of plated food in the intersection of Opportunity and Weaknesses. This intersection is the internal development strategy so the action is to convert weakness to strengths and one way of doing that is to purchase plates, cutlery, and invest in dishwashers and kitchen space.

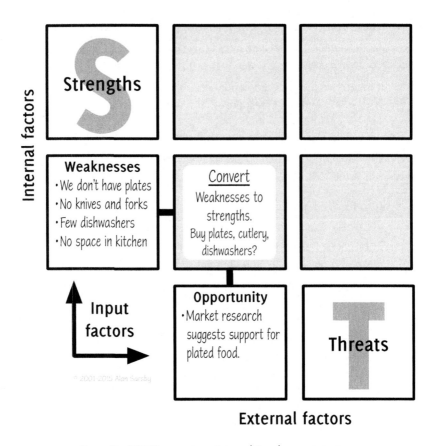

Figure 9: TOWS suggests an Internal Development strategy

An uncritical application of SWOT and TOWS would suggest investment in cutlery, plates and a supportive menu. Both front-of-house and back-of-house would require some investment. Front-of-house would require crockery and cutlery, as well as waiting staff to clear and collect plates, knives and forks; these staff would also need training. Back-of-house would need a dishwasher (with staff training, cleaning materials, water softeners, and so on), and storage. Cutlery becomes lost, crockery is broken, so consequently prices might need to increase. With sit-down meals, customers are likely to stay longer, so the Basic Burger Bar would need to rethink the seating capacity.

Context is important here: The Basic Burger Bar attracts low-spending customers who stay for a relatively short time. The front-of-house and back-of-house procedures are optimised towards this behaviour. Against this context, plated meals are inconsistent with the operating mode of the Basic Burger Bar.

If the managers of the Basic Burger Bar wanted to take advantage of the plated food opportunity, they should consider opening a new restaurant with a different operating ethos, and a new SWOT analysis.

7 Reviewing your strategy

7.1 Summary

At this point you have the essential theory to prepare a strategy using the SWOT/TOWS technique.

The core SWOT framework, its conversion to TOWS, and the analytical tools of match and convert have been introduced. The importance of a context and purpose have been emphasised as being vital to a successful analysis.

The example of the Basic Burger Bar provides a straightforward, if simplistic, situation. In reality, decision-making is more difficult and decisions often involve some degree of subjectivity. Remember, an important benefit of SWOT analysis is the conversations among the organisation's decision-makers.

7.2 Testing a strategy

Before final decisions are it is important to review the feasibility of what the analysis suggests. There are many ways of testing a strategy. The following list provides an indication of the kind of tests that could be used; the list would vary depending on the context and purpose of the analysis.

- Is the strategy appropriate for your business sector/sub-sector? In business jargon this is often referred to as the *business fit*.

- Does the strategy align with the business' ethics and values?

- Is the strategy an incremental change, or is it a fundamental shift?

- Effectiveness — does the strategy deliver an advantage or distinction?

- What are the costs for the strategy? What resources are needed for implementation? Are the benefits of the strategy worth the costs?

- Would the strategic action be reliable and sustainable?

- Is it possible to visualise what things would be like after the strategic change has been implemented? Being able to do this helps one to communicate the decision, and to encourage the motivation for the change.

- Is the strategy and solution elegant?

- What would happen if you do nothing?

7.3   Deployment

Your strategy must be converted from intent into action. Strategy deployment is a full subject in its own right and beyond the scope of this book. Four themes to consider when preparing for strategy deployment are:

Approvals from key stakeholders
Any kind of change needs the buy-in from key stakeholders.

Communication
How to communicate your strategy — the goals for communication are well known: clarity, simplicity, consistency, and self-adjusting so people can internalise the message in their own way.

Implementation
Implementing a strategy often involves a change programme of some kind. Give some thought as to what kind of programme, and how big it might be.

Measuring success
How would you know whether your strategy has been a success? Give some thought to the kind of indicators or measures you would need so that you can check that the advantage or distinction is delivering real results.

Part 3 — Case study examples

8   Examples and case studies

Case studies are one way of illustrating how the theory can be applied to real situations. The examples provided here cover four different areas of business activity and one personal one to give you a feel for the variety of topics that could go into a SWOT/TOWS developed strategy. As with all case studies, they represent a snapshot of a situation.

Each case study includes the context and purpose with a list of factors and their location on a SWOT/TOWS diagram.

8.1   Case study: The coffee shop

This is a favourite example in further education and it is included here because of that popularity.

Take care with examples like these because you can only account for what you see as an *external observer* — that is, the things you experience by visiting the coffee shop and their competitors (often only a few steps away on the high street). You could use information such as their report and accounts and these might provide you with some additional inputs for the SWOT. However, you are limited in what you can know about the economic model of the coffee shop industry and their internal processes, so it is difficult to judge what is a Strength or a Weakness; hence you can only produce a generalised SWOT.

If you are given an assignment which might lead to a generalised SWOT analysis, consider a benchmarking approach. For example, compare and contrast the coffee shop to a nearby alternative coffee shop.

[Context] The coffee shop is a bespoke high-street café selling coffee beverages (and coffee variations) together with snack-sized pastries. The high street coffee shop industry is very competitive with other global and national operators. At 2015 prices, a typical customer spends £6 – £8 on an eat-in visit or slightly less on a 'to-go' visit. A repeat customer visiting twice a day (breakfast and lunch) over one hundred days per year is worth over £1,000 per year in revenue.

The café is located in a prime retail site within a busy shopping park and attracts substantial passing trade. Competitors' local cafés (branded international franchises) are a short walk away.

The bean used in the coffee product is Robusta *(coffea canephora)*, which is rich in caffeine. However, market research has identified that discerning coffee drinkers prefer other beans, in particular Arabica *(coffea arabica)*, which is reputed to be more refined and aromatic. Local competitors are advertising *100% Arabica* and are successfully attracting these discerning customers.

[Purpose] To review the use of the Robusta bean in the coffee beverages and consider changing the recipe to use arabica beans.

[Social] Customers are becoming more concerned with the ethics of coffee production. It is a widely held view that the coffee growers receive poor payment for the value of their crop. The rise of ethical brands causes some customers to go elsewhere. Some competitors distinguish their establishment by promoting ethical sources.

[Economics] Robusta is cheaper to grow and more abundant, consequently the input costs are lower than Arabica.

[Technological] The espresso machines (grinding, packing, pressure) can take either bean.

Recording the factors and developing the responses on a SWOT/TOWS diagram results in something like Figure 10.

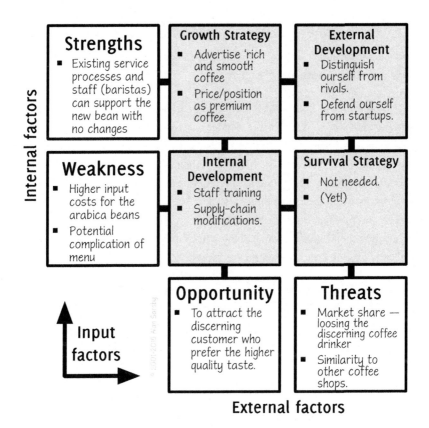

Figure 10: TOWS diagram for the review of coffee bean

Note — The ethical brand supplies issue is a parallel SWOT/TOWS analysis.

Exercises

1 — Next time you go to a coffee shop, observe what is going on and create your own SWOT/TOWS analysis.
Would you change the coffee bean?

2 — Imagine you wanted to start a new coffee shop business. What would your SWOT/TOWS analysis contain?

8.2 Case study: A charity facing total loss of revenue

This case study illustrates the impact of a change in government policy on an organisation's purpose and existence.

The organisation is in the care sector and provides support for people with learning disabilities. Traditionally, services were commissioned by local government agencies using block contracts with care providers to deliver standard levels of service. The big shift in their business environment was the political objective to pay benefits directly to the beneficiary. The beneficiary would now be an *Individual Budget* holder. And together with their circle of friends and family, could choose what support they need, from whom they like, rather than their benefit money being administered on their behalf by the local authority's block contracts with care providers.

If this organisation had followed the 'do-nothing' option, the block contracts would eventually expire and the steady-state revenue would wind-down. Within approximately 12 to 18 months the block-contract based revenue would reduce to zero. (And as a consequence, risk closing the business.)

[Context] The charity is in the care sector; their charitable objective is to provide support and help for people with learning disabilities. The charity has a turnover of £100 million (2012).

[Purpose] To examine how Individual Budgets impacts their care business, and decide how to respond to the government's new objective.

[Political] The provision of care has traditionally been accessed and administered through local authorities, who would then commission a service provider to deliver the care service package using a block contract.

[Political] Government policy is to change the economic model so that a person in need of care would receive the resources (as money) directly instead of it being channelled through the local authority.

[Economic] The economic model of the care sector would change from wholesale provision (for example, the block contract) to that where the person in need of support would be a retail customer of the care provider. The flow of resources and money would be entirely different; consequently existing strengths in bids and tenders, largely a wholesale model of provision, are no longer relevant.

[Threat] Most of the charity's revenue comes via local government. In the near future none of it will.

[Opportunity] People with an Individual Budget holders are going to be the new paying customers. These individuals often have what is known as a 'circle of support' so the opportunity is to present the charity as the provider of choice to their circle of support and to the individual budget holder.

[Strength] The charity has a good track record of delivering care and has considerable positive feedback from the people it supports.

[Weakness] The charity's former strength of being able to respond to local authority requirements in bids and tenders is no longer relevant.

[Weakness] Employees do not have retail sales skills.

[Weakness] The charity has no retail-oriented process for an individual budget holder and their circle of support to make a purchase.

[Weakness] The charity has no supporting infrastructure, for example computer systems to support sales enquiries, and thus no management information to help operational decision-making.

[Weakness] Individual service components are often incorporated within a larger package of services. The client might not need, nor want, the whole package of services.

Using PESTEL and SWOT has highlighted many factors. Positioning these on a SWOT/ TOWS diagram would look something like Figure 11.

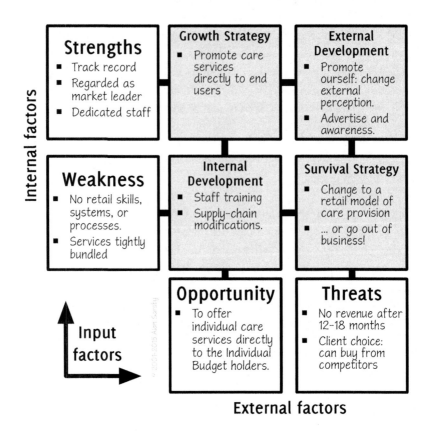

Figure 11: Care Sector SWOT/TOWS

Whilst the foregoing paints a desperate picture for the charity, it demonstrates that in the old environment they were the market leader. Suddenly, in the new environment, they might not even be in business!

For this case, the SWOT/TOWS analysis led to a *Strategic Imperative*.

Strategic Imperative

> In the words of the Executive Director:
> *"Unless we change the way we do business, and make ourselves attractive to the retail buyer of personal care services, we will go out of business within a year."*

The SWOT/TOWS analysis shows the need for a survival strategy. The goal is to *convert* the Threat into an Opportunity; and to convert existing weaknesses into new strengths.

Strategy and actions

Survival

- Re-invent our organisation as a retail provider of care services. In order to do this …

Internal Development

- Convert — unbundle our services so each element can be individually priced and sold.

- Develop a retail customer service journey from initial enquiry, enquiry tracking, order taking (sales), and fulfilment (service delivery).

- Train our staff in customer service and sales skills.

- Develop the financial systems for retail sales.

External Development

- Develop and promote the organisation — advertise directly to the new Individual Budget Holders and to their family and friends.

- Awareness — advertise and host seminars aimed at both family and friends, and advisors of care services.

Growth

Develop related services for other groups with similar (but different) conditions. For example, retail care services for those with autism or dementia.

8.3   Case study: Self-employment — starting a new business

This case study demonstrates the use of SWOT/TOWS for a personal goal. It also illustrates that soft factors can have a significant impact on the strategic actions. This case study can be adapted for applying for employment.

[Context] Kay is currently employed as the operations manager of a contract cleaning business. The company's business includes large-scale cleaning services, for example cleaning school premises during the vacations, or builder's cleans (cleaning a house immediately following the builder's completion of their work so it is ready for use or marketing).

On the downside, the company is a family business whose directors are reluctant to share their rewards. Employee satisfaction is consistently low with many disciplinary cases (often for trivial 'offences') and there is poor communication between the directors and the operational teams. Against this background Kay is considering setting up a limited company to become self-employed.

[Purpose] Define a strategy for Kay to start a new contract cleaning company.

[Opportunity] Several clients have indicated that they would switch their allegiance to Kay if she were to start her own contract cleaning business.

[Political/Legal] New regulations are about to come into force which require cleaning staff to be adequately trained. (To BICS[1] standards.)

[Threat] If Kay were to leave, there is a small possibility that her existing employer requires a non-compete agreement. The risk is small since the matter is vague in her contract of employment.

[Threat] Whilst some existing clients support Kay, others, typically the larger corporations might not, because the effort of reworking their procurement processes could be an unnecessary expense, for example, due diligence, supplier qualification and supplier management.

---

1 BICS - British Institute of Cleaning Science.

[Strengths] Kay's expertise includes surface, wall, and floor cleaning using specialist industrial solvents, and project logistics to source cleaning operators to the client's site.

[Weakness] Kay has limited skills in running a business, as distinct from operations management in the cleaning industry, and no skills in starting a new business. Additionally, there is insufficient cash in her savings to purchase the amount of equipment and supplies required to start the business.

Placing these factors on a SWOT/TOWS diagram would result in something like Figure 12.

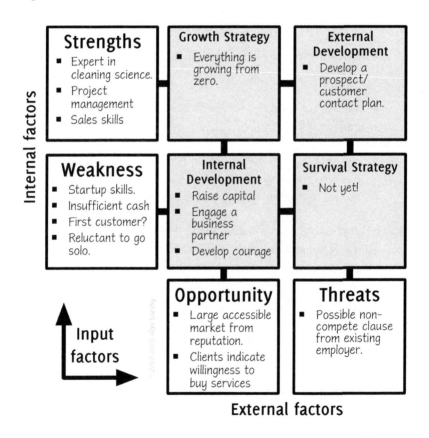

Figure 12: SWOT/TOWS for Kay's ambition to start a new company

Strategy and actions

The most obvious strategy is survival because the threats and weaknesses strongly intersect. She can either put up with the problematic employer, or leave. Let's assume that Kay wants to start her own business; the primary strategy type is Internal Development because the opportunities are there.

A strategy based on Internal Development could include:

- Raise working capital to purchase tools and equipment.

- Purchase tools (floor scrubbers, vacuum cleaners), materials (cleaning chemistry, consumables) and other equipment.

- Establish the business as a business — company formation, web site, telecoms and computing, and so on.

- Manage cash reserves to cover cash flow from the period of the first contract through to being paid.

- Engage a business partner with experience in establishing small businesses, and complementary services for the cleaning industry such as training design and delivery.

The one weakness is Kay's reluctance to take a leap into the unknown; the perceived risk of failure is too high. The most important strategic action is finding emotional support to help her through the first steps of creating a new business and becoming self-employed; this is the most important element in Kay's strategy. Actions could include:

- Taking the small preparatory steps in advance of resigning from her current employer.

- Seeking support and advice from local business links.

Note that the other quadrants in the TOWS framework have been ignored at this stage. One cannot have a Growth Strategy until there is a business to grow; one cannot have External Development without a business (this area has been covered to some extent by some customers indicating their willingness to engage Kay). The main point from this case study is that strategy is not mechanical and must also incorporate the human and emotional factors.

8.4　Case study: Wi-Fi in a fast food restaurant

We introduced the Basic Burger Bar in §6.2 where the opportunity to serve plated food was strategically declined. In this case study, we'll add a new aspect to the study — the provision of free Wi-Fi in the restaurant so that customers can use their own computing devices (laptops, tablets, phones) to check email, surf the web and so on.

The context needs extending to embrace more of the social culture of the restaurant, and the purpose needs to be modified.

[Context] The Basic Burger Bar is a fast food restaurant. The duration that a customer might be in the restaurant is short: The duration from entry, ordering, paying, eating, clearing and leaving is unlikely to be longer than 30 minutes.

The environment is designed to reflect these short duration visits: The décor is garish, the noise level is high, and seats are designed for ease of cleaning not for comfort.

[Purpose] Decide whether to offer a free Wi-Fi service in the Basic Burger Bar.

[Threat] Loss of Customers: Observation of customer attendance and exit surveys indicate that some are frequenting nearby competitors who offer free Wi-Fi for their customers to use whilst on the premises.

[Threat] Reputation: risk being seen as out of touch and unattractive to the mobile computing generation.

[Opportunity] To retain our customers.

[Weakness] Encouraging long-stay customers is inconsistent with the ethos of fast-food/quick-to-enter, quick-to-depart. There is insufficient table space to hold the net increase in occupants.

[Weakness] Although central IT skills can undertake the provision, there are no front-of-house technical support skills. Most staff are not technically knowledgeable and their jobs have low skill requirements. Giving a customer technical support would deflect their attention away from their core job function and be inconsistent with the notion of 'fast.'

Placing these factors on a SWOT/TOWS diagram results in something like Figure 13.

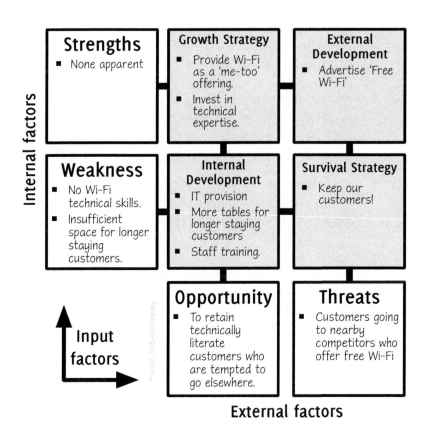

Figure 13: SWOT/TOWS for Wi-Fi in Basic Burger Bar

Strategy review

The main driver for change is to keep customers from drifting away to competitors. The threat is exacerbated by important weaknesses. The strategic action is:

- Convert the Threat into an Opportunity — to attract the technology-literate customers.

- Invest in External Development by advertising to inform prospective customers that Wi-Fi is available for free in the Basic Burger Bar.

- Convert the Weakness into a Strength — Invest in Wi-Fi, staff training.

- Internal Development: Create a fair use Wi-Fi service policy, for example to cover how long a customer may stay connected. Creation of self-help support for customers for Wi-Fi users.

Note — this type of strategy is a catch-up action; also known as a 'me-too' response so that your distinction of being the 'laggard' is averted. It doesn't provide you with a new feature to distinguish yourself, rather it prevents the drain of customers to competitors.

Exercise:

Reposition the *lack* of Wi-Fi as an Opportunity (conversion from a Threat). Consider a strategy to support the notion of a *Quiet Coffee Café* as an opportunity, and hence attract a different type of cliental. Perform a swot/tows analysis on the Quiet Coffee Café.

9 Summary

SWOT can be applied to a wide variety of issues and problems. But, like all tools it is dependent on the skill of the user. So, let's conclude with a checklist to help you prepare a SWOT based strategy:

- Be clear what the four boxes in SWOT actually mean. The two axes in control (internal or external) and impact (helpful or harmful) define what should be recorded in each box.

- Be clear of the situation — the context and what problem is being addressed. See § 5.1 and §6.2.
  Sometimes, several SWOTs are required to consider multiple issues.

- SWOT captures input factors. You might need several methods of identifying the input factors. See §5.4 and those suggested in Appendix 2 and Appendix 3.

- Apply the Match and Convert principles to connect internal/external factors to the corresponding helpful/harmful factors and thus discover a possible strategy. See §3.

- The TOWS suggests the *type* of strategy appropriate to the mixture of input factors. See §4.

- Remember to examine the strategies in order to check that they fit with the realities and characteristics of the business. See §7.

Part 4 — Appendixes

Appendix 1 — Alternative drawings of SWOT

Although SWOT is commonly drawn as 4-boxes in a 2×2 grid, there are other representations, the form shown in Figure 14 emphasises the internal/external aspects of SWOT.

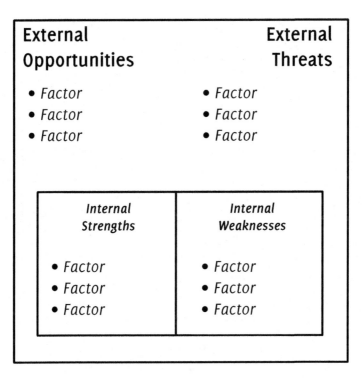

Figure 14: An earlier representation of SWOT

A stylised version of SWOT is shown in Figure 15.

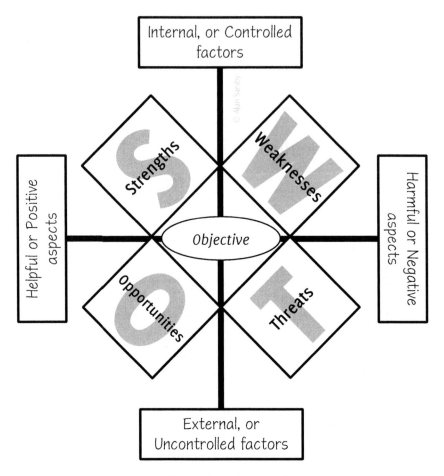

Figure 15: A stylised drawing of SWOT

!	If you are feeling artistic (and why not!) The squares can be replaced with other shapes — pentagons and heptagons seem popular. But take care; a cloud shape is visually incongruent with the harmful factors — fluffy clouds might be soft and cuddly, but threats can be sharp and dangerous.

Alternative names for the four quadrants

The names of the four quadrants have alternatives. Some find the language of SWOT too war-like. And in a world littered with political correctness, for some the choice of word carries more weight than the meaning.

For example:

Strengths — some interpret this in the context of a *warrior* and strength of an army.
Alternatives include *Advantages* or *Supporting Factors*.

Weakness — some people (and certain professions and cultures) object to this because it implies *inadequate* or *shortcoming*.
Alternatives include *Liabilities*, *Challenges*, or *Areas for Development*.

Opportunities — this term is frequently derided by two camps: those who see the world in a deterministic way and hence dislike opportunism, and those who see this as opportunistic exploitation.
Alternatives include *options*, *openings*, or *attractions*.

Threats — to some this has overtones of violence or the headlines used in the tabloid press. However, in swot the Threats are vitally important in the recognition of, and response to, external hazards. Downgrading the terminology with casual or softer vocabulary is likely to lead to indecisive thinking and a poor strategy.
Alternatives include *hazards*, or *risks*.

Although it might be attractive from a politically-correct point of view, presenting new terminology to your tutor might disrupt their thought flow, and hence their propensity to give you higher marks.

Appendix 2— PESTEL: discovery of external factors

PESTEL is a tool for identifying the Opportunities and Threats for SWOT analysis. PESTEL is an acronym where each letter indicates an aspect of factors that could influence both your internal practices and your external products and services. Some aspects, such as Health and Safety might fall under several headings; that is to be expected.

Political — Political factors are those coming from government. Political factors include:
Policy direction — the intention and opinion of governments and their view of how a nation functions, and its role within the community (local, national and global). Policies in this context are about a government's intentions, including:
Law-making — the type and style of laws that a government promotes and introduces;
Taxation — the principles of government revenue collection; and
Budgetary — how the government intends to spend the tax revenue.

Economic — Economic factors are those relating to the economy at large. Economic factors include those led by a government, for example interest rates, the amount of money in circulation, national debt, and so on. These factors also include those that exist within industry or commercial sectors. For example, the economic model for double-decker busses is different from that of domestic saloon cars; the economic model for the self-employed is different from that of a publicly listed company.

Social — Social factors might include healthcare, culture and arts, law and order, and population and demographics.

Technological — Technological factors can be broad-ranging, including everything from automation in factories and offices, information technology in key operational processes, and research and development.

Environmental — Environmental in PESTEL includes ecological factors such as air quality, nature and waste disposal. For example, the Waste Electrical and Electronic Equipment (WEEE) regulations caused substantial product redesign or withdrawal.

Legal — Legal factors include laws, regulations and statutory requirements. These affect both what you do and how you do it.

Figure 16 illustrates PESTEL when it is used for an environmental scan.

If a PESTEL factor is relevant, your SWOT analysis should include statements of how a factor is observed or experienced at three levels. The levels should provide a logical progression from the big picture (macro) to the specific. These levels are:

- Macro — The factor as it applies everywhere;

- Sector — The factor as it applies to your market sector; and

- Specific — How the factor impacts on your specific organisation.

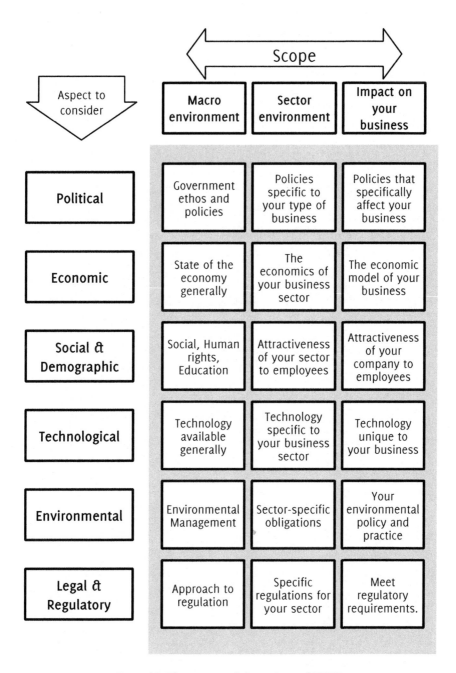

Figure 16: The scope and dimensions of PESTEL

You might encounter different variants and acronyms, see below. These all do similar jobs of reminding you *where to look* when doing the environmental scan, and can be useful tool when brainstorming.

Acronym	Meaning
PESTLE/ PESTEL	Political, Economic, Social, Technological, Legal, Environmental
PEST	Political, Economic, Social, Technological
PESTLIED	Political, Economic, Socio-Cultural, Technological, Legal, International, Environmental, Demographic
STEEPLE	Social (including demographic), Technological, Economic, Environmental, Political, Legal, Ethical
SLEPT	Socio-cultural, Legal, Economic, Political, Technological
LoNG-PESTLE	Local, National, and Global additions to PESTLE

Appendix 3 — Identifying Strengths and Weaknesses

Strengths and Weaknesses are internal factors. There are many ways to identify these factors; here are three suggestions that you might employ.

1 Process-mapping

Process mapping is a technique used to diagnose the functions of an organisation. This mapping starts from an external point of view, and records what happens along the way to the service being fulfilled.

Process mapping is not the view of the service provider; it is the view of the process user or process customer.

The method is to start with a beneficiary, for example the customer, and follow what happens at each stage of their experience. This approach is often recorded as an informal diagram. This technique is also known as the *staple yourself to ...* method. For example, a weakness could be the slow response to purchase orders, then mentally staple yourself to a purchase order and follow its journey through the organisation. Beware, the temptation with this process-mapping approach can be to record the mechanics and resources (for example, headcount); for SWOT, the purpose is to observe where the issue (Threat or Opportunity) is supported (Strength) or hindered (Weakness) by the presence, absence, or performance, of internal capabilities. The key benefit of this approach is that you will have a diagram of how things work currently.

> Note — In management consultancy jargon, the current state is known as the *as-is* situation. When things have to change, a similar diagram known as the *To-Be* state is created and the differences between the *as-is* and *to-be* are the foundations of a change plan.

2   What if ...

The *What if* method deliberately injects a big idea (sometimes known as a BHAG — Big Hairy Audacious Goal) into the analysis. For example, *What if* we discontinue accepting payment by cash and only accept payments by card; *What if* we engage a public relations company; *What if* we made our products exclusively for left-handed customers; *What if* our key supplier becomes bankrupt, and so on. For SWOT, the Strengths and Weaknesses to support or hinder the BHAG become apparent as the big idea is worked through.

The advantage of the *What If* approach is that it encourages creativity and freethinking. Where process-mapping is useful for analysing and responding to previously identified issues, *What If* engages issues and topics that have not yet appeared on the horizon.

> Note — Within the context of mobile computing, an opportunity for a hand-held computer was envisaged. *Process-mapping* led to smaller and cheaper laptop computers known as netbooks. *What if* led to a new category of computing — the tablet.

3   Business function checklist

Using checklists, or tick lists, is a method of ensuring that a wide variety of factors are not forgotten and have been taken into account. For SWOT, checklists are a convenient way of reminding you *where to look* for strengths and weaknesses. Typically, a checklist could be created using the major functions of an organisation. These might include:

Customer-facing activities

- Marketing/Advertising/Public relations/
- Customer service/customer experience
- Sales, pricing, product attractiveness
- Delivery and fulfilment
- Payments, receipting

Financial and investors

- Banking
- Reconciliation
- Tax management — returns and settlements
- Investor relations

People — staff, volunteers, employees

- Selection and recruitment (Hire and fire)
- Morale, motivation, loyalty, remuneration
- Capabilities of leaders and managers (Staff development)

Research and development

- New product development
- Ability to experiment, prototype, test, pilot

Resource management

- Capability of Management Information Systems
- Knowledge management
- Quality systems

Operations

- Marketing, promotion, awareness
- Sales, order-taking
- Shipping and fulfilment, Goods inward
- Storage, logistics

Resources

- Plant, machinery, tools, methods and techniques, people
- Information, Communications and Technology (ICT)

Appendix 4— Planning and organising your assignment

In further and higher education, the scope of business studies, strategy topics often include the SWOT technique, either as analysis or as a strategy development tool.

Popular SWOT assignments usually take one of two forms:

1   Go to a coffee bar (or similar retail establishment) and 'do' a SWOT analysis on the business. These assignments are prone to many potential errors which affect your results and potentially your assignment score. Reflecting the popularity of the coffee shop assignments, refer to the case studies and the suggested workarounds to avoid the error-prone nature of these analyses.
A variation of the field trip to a coffee bar is to be given a specific business such as a well-known technology company or a well-known supermarket, and perform a remote SWOT analysis. This might require research into publicly available information (for example Internet searches) or a library search to discover the factors which make up a SWOT analysis.

2   Read a case study from which you extract the factors for a SWOT analysis.

- In Higher Education you might be offered a placement in an organisation as if you were an external business consultant who is performing a strategy review.

- You might include a SWOT analysis within another project, for example, a dissertation on energy efficient housing might include a SWOT analysis.

> Just a cautious note: commercial organisations don't often publish their strategy; for a strategy to be successful it is desirable to hide it from the competition. What you read might be watered down statements that sound good but don't stand much scrutiny.

Planning and organising your assignment

Figure 17 below is an outline which demonstrates a way to undertake a SWOT assignment.

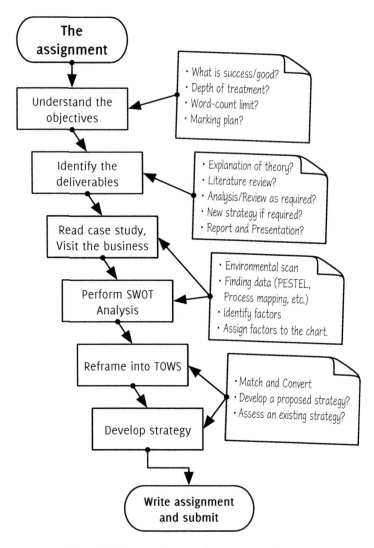

Figure 17: Suggested approach to a SWOT assignment

Appendix 5— A significant waste of time?

SWOT is often misused: starting in the wrong place, being over congratulatory about strengths, and dismissive (denial) concerning threats, and failing to convert the analysis into actionable objectives. These have led to some labelling SWOT as a *Significant Waste Of Time.*

A major source of wasted effort arises when SWOT is applied as a general activity without a specific focus. At the time of writing an Internet search for "SWOT + Apple" produced more than 49 <u>million</u> hits! The page one results were generalised SWOTs with little substance and no analysis. A similar search "SWOT + iphone + android" — produced 1.6 million hits — many were quite specific but only included what could be observed as an outsider. Many of the so-called facts were guesses and assumptions; be careful about the intrinsic quality of the factors you collect.

The following five suggestions should help you avoid the significant waste of time:

- Draw SWOT or TOWS with x and y axes labelled this helps you position the factors in the correct box.

- Clarify and state the purpose of the analysis. This help you identify which factor goes where.

- Start with Threats or Opportunities. Avoid the temptation to start with strengths. Until the threats or opportunities have been identified with regard to the objective, you don't yet know weather an internal factor should be positioned as a strength or a weakness.

- Finish the analysis with a business-fit/reality test.

- If the assignment traps you into a 'do a SWOT on a coffee shop' or similar situation, consider using a benchmarking approach such as comparing and contrasting two similar organisations.

Appendix 6 — History and citations

The history of SWOT is not as clear as one might hope for and consequently references and citations need careful consideration.

Some writers suggest that SWOT was created by Albert Humphrey[1]. His work certainly has the foundations, but does not use the terminology as SWOT. His article (p16 *ff*) uses the vocabulary and concepts of stakeholder, goals, market opportunity, competence, and resources. Later (p27 *ff*) speaks of business environment and strengths and weaknesses. It appears that the foundations of SWOT are there, but a diagram or matrix is not given, and neither is the acronym.

Some authors, Thakur [7], claim that SWOT is a derivation of SOFT. Soft is Satisfactory, Opportunities, Faults (or Failures) and Threats.

Swot is often cited in the classic works, for example Johnson and Scholes [2]. However, the origins are not given, and SWOT is assumed to exist *a priori*. SWOT is mentioned in §3.6.2 (p134) in approximately one-hundred words. It is applied to a case study in illustration 4.8 (p182). Strengths and Weaknesses are given a longer treatment (p183, approximately 250 words). A further treatment is given in Illustration 8.5 (p387) where using SWOT identifies some strategic options which are ranked against the strategic factors.

Compendium strategy books, for example Key Management Models, van Assen et al [3] chapter 15 introduces the SWOT model without citations. The text moves quickly into TOWS and then introduces a prioritisation approach which they designate as the confrontation matrix.
Likewise Hardin and Long [4] chapter 40 (p187–190) outline SWOT using a diagram similar to Figure 14. They reference Johnson and Scholes [2].

SWOT does not enjoy universal popularity; Hill and Westbrook [5] consider that major failings include excessive factors, generalised work, and the lack of prioritisation. They famously claim that "SWOT is due for a product recall".

On the other hand, Weihrich [6] considers that SWOT should be extended and proposed the TOWS framework as a means of identifying options and actions that respond to the factors.

Bibliography

[1]   Learned, P.E., Christensen,C.R., Andrews, K.R., Guth, W.D. *Business Policy — Text and Cases.* 1969, Irwin Inc., Illinois, USA.

[2]   Johnson, G., Scholes K., *Exploring Corporate Strategy*, 6th Ed., 2002, Person Education.

[3]   Van Assen, M., Van den Berg, G., & Pietersma, P. (2009), *Key Management Models: The 60+ models every manager needs to know.* Pearson Education.

[4]   Harding S. Long T., *MBA Management Models*, 1998, Gower Publishing.

[5]   Hill, T. and Westbrook, R., *SWOT analysis: its time for a product recall, Long Range Planning*, vol. 30, no. 1 (1997), pp. 46–52.

[6]   Winerick, Heinz. *The TOWS Matrix — A Tool for Situational Analysis,* Downloaded 2016-02-06 from http://www.rillo.ee/docs/2008/Weichrich_LRP_1982.pdf

[7]   Thakur, Sidharth, *A History of the SWOT Analysis*, downloaded 2014-12-06 http://www.brighthubpm.com/methods-strategies/99629-history-of-the-swot-analysis/

Additional resources

Free resources accompany this book and are downloadable for use by buyers of this book. Point your browser to www.leading-swot.uk then follow the links to downloadable resources.

Almost all the diagrams used in this work are included in the download. These are in common industry standard file formats, including Microsoft PowerPoint (.ppt), Apple Keynote, (.key) and Scalable Vector Graphic (.svg). Further resources might be added in due course. To receive notifications, consider signing up to the mailing list. It is a low volume list and you can unsubscribe at any time.

Bespoke resources:

If you have a need for bespoke resources please let us know via email to editor@leadership-library.co.uk

Bespoke resources related to SWOT could include: customised versions of this book incorporating your own company's procedures; branded resources for use in workshops, and similar materials.
In-house training events, team meetings, or similar events, can also be arranged.

Your feedback:

If this book has helped with your assignment, we'd be delighted if you'd let us know. Alternatively, consider posting a review on the site where you obtained this book.

If you have suggested improvements, it would be good to know those too.

And if you have ideas for similar subject matter, please send us an email.

editor@leadership-library.co.uk

Many thanks, and good luck with your assignment.

About the author

Alan Sarsby has enjoyed over forty years in many different careers, initially in electronic engineering and IT strategy then later in customer service and business change. He has developed and implemented novel approaches to enterprise design and change leadership. Since 2001, Alan has specialised in training services. He is a conference speaker and non-fiction author.

Alan Sarsby, Bachelor of Technology (hons), MIET.

Alan may be able to help you with:

- Training, seminars, conference speaking,

- Consulting services,

- Customised versions of this of this book to incorporate your own organisation's policies and procedures.

Please contact Spectaris Ltd, on 01449 711048, or by email to editor@leadership-library.co.uk

—Δ—

Printed in Great Britain
by Amazon

12504938R00051